ON YOUR WAY TO SUCCEEDING WITH THE MASTERS®
THEORY BOOK

By HELEN MARLAIS with PEGGY O'DELL

About the Theory Book

On Your Way to Succeeding with the Masters® Theory Book correlates with the repertoire collection, *On Your Way to Succeeding with the Masters®*.

For each keyboard piece found in *On Your Way to Succeeding with the Masters®*, a particular concept is "spotlighted" in the *Theory Book*. Examples are whole and half steps, five-finger patterns, tonic and dominant, major scales, accidentals, form, key signatures, triads, motives, etc. Composition and improvisation activities are found throughout the book. These develop the students' understanding of each theoretical concept and encourage student engagement in the learning process. Having students work with the various concepts in several different ways assists them with the retention of this important information and enables them to build on this solid foundation.

It is not necessary for students using the *Theory Book* to start at the beginning and study all of the pieces in order to understand the concepts. Since each piece spotlights a different concept, this makes it possible to start anywhere in the book and study the desired pieces in any order! In addition to the concept that is "spotlighted" with each piece, there is a *Glossary of Musical Terms* at the back of the book (starting on page 68) for the student's reference.

Using the repertoire in *On Your Way to Succeeding with the Masters®* in conjunction with this *Theory Book* will prepare students for the works of the master composers found in *Succeeding with the Masters®*, *Volume One*. Each different *Succeeding with the Masters®* book gives students a historical perspective so that they understand the life and times of each era they are learning, along with valuable practice strategies for every piece. The series also includes a supplemental *Student Activity Book* for each era.

Production: Frank J. Hackinson
Production Coordinators: Joyce Loke and Satish Bhakta
Cover: Terpstra Design, San Francisco
Cover Art Concept: Helen Marlais
Engraving: Tempo Music Press, Inc.
Printer: Tempo Music Press, Inc.

ISBN-13: 978-1-56939-826-5

TABLE OF CONTENTS

Medieval Era (c. 675–c. 1430)

Trouvère

Richard I, Coeur-de-lion
(1157–1199)
arr. Helen Marlais

Spotlight on Half and Whole Steps

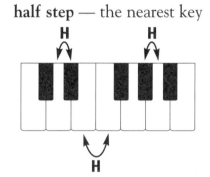

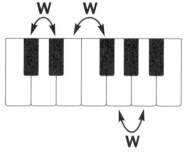

Mark the half and whole steps in measures 2 and 3. The first one is done for you.

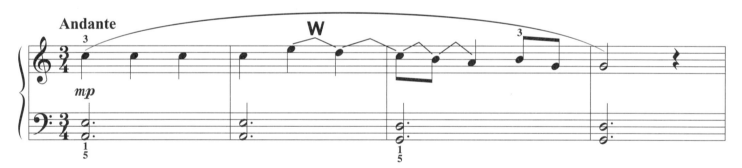

Mark the half and whole steps in measures 10 and 11. The first one is done for you.

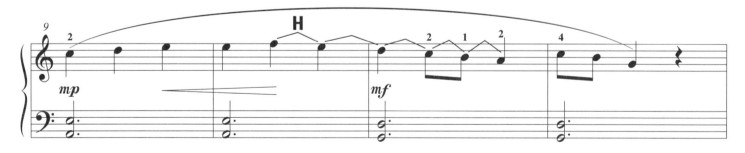

Except for the last measure, the L.H. uses the same interval throughout the piece.
Place a check by the name of this interval.

_____ 5th

_____ 4th

The tempo of this piece is *Andante*. Place a check by its meaning.

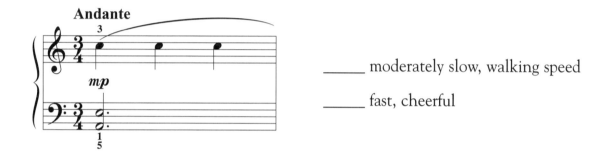

_____ moderately slow, walking speed

_____ fast, cheerful

Write in the counting for the measures below.

Place a check by the letter name of the L.H. staff note in the last measure.

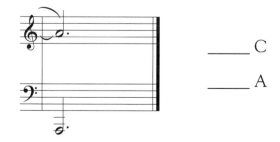

_____ C

_____ A

Ballade

Perrin d'Angicourt
(fl. 1245–1270)
arr. Helen Marlais

Spotlight on Intervals

interval — the distance between two notes.

2nd   4th   7th

Name the intervals in the L.H. for measures 5-8. Place a check next to the correct answer.

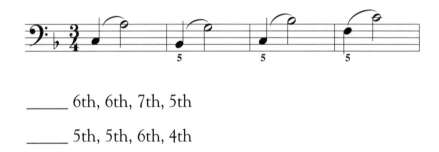

_____ 6th, 6th, 7th, 5th

_____ 5th, 5th, 6th, 4th

Name the key signature. Place a check next to the correct answer.

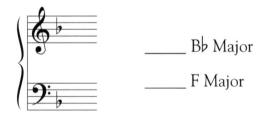

_____ B♭ Major

_____ F Major

What is the meaning of the term *dolce* in measure 1? _____

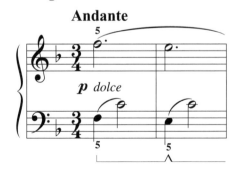

Andante

p dolce

FJH2100

In the R.H., there are at least three things that are different between lines 1 and 3. List them.

Line 1:

Line 3:

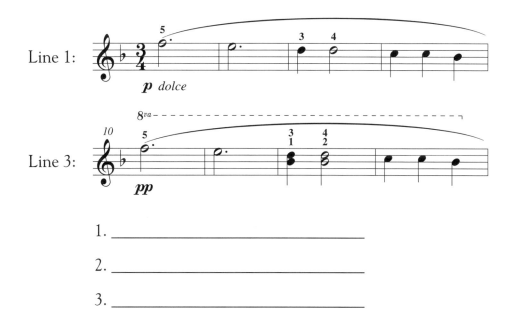

1. _____

2. _____

3. _____

The R.H. notes in measures 1-8 belong to what **Major** scale? _____

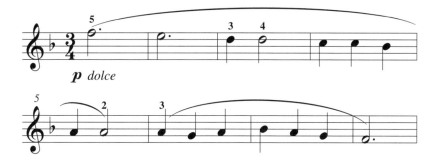

Composition

1. Finish the R.H. in measures 3-4 below.
2. Use any notes from the d minor five-finger pattern.
3. Write in the counting between the staffs.
4. Play your composition to make sure you like it.

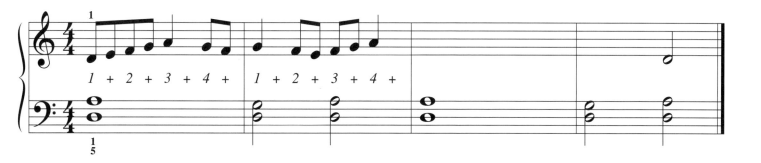

Renaissance Era (c. 1430–c. 1600)

PAVANE
from *Sixième livre de danceries*

Claude Gervaise
(fl. 1540–1560)
arr. Helen Marlais

Spotlight on Five-Finger Patterns

five-finger pattern — 5 notes in consecutive steps. It is named after the lowest note.

Major five-finger pattern —
all whole steps except there is a half step
between the third and fourth notes.

minor five-finger pattern —
all whole steps except there is a half step
between the second and third notes.

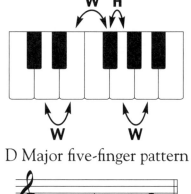

D Major five-finger pattern

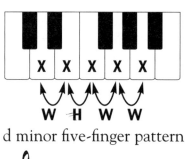

d minor five-finger pattern

Place a check next to the correct answers below.

In measures 5 and 6, what is the name of the circled five-finger pattern?

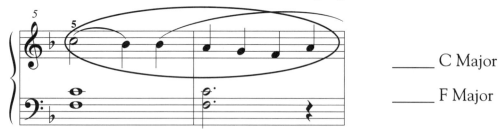

_____ C Major

_____ F Major

In measures 6, 7, and 8, what is the name of the circled five-finger pattern?

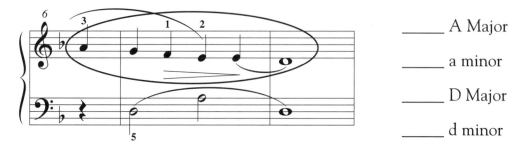

_____ A Major

_____ a minor

_____ D Major

_____ d minor

Place a check next to the correct answers below.

The *Andante* tempo marking means:

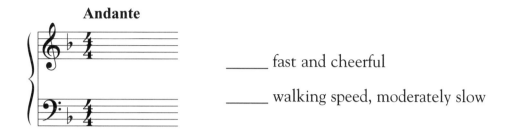

_____ fast and cheerful

_____ walking speed, moderately slow

The name of the key signature is:

_____ F Major

_____ G Major

The name of the accidental in measure 15 is:

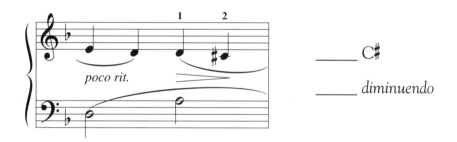

_____ C♯

_____ *diminuendo*

The dynamic sign ⟌ in measure 7 means:

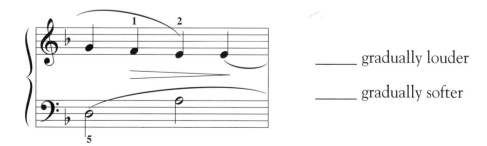

_____ gradually louder

_____ gradually softer

A Study in $\frac{5}{4}$ Time
Thomas Morley
(1558–1602)

Spotlight on Time Signatures

These are **time signatures**: $\frac{2}{4}$ $\frac{3}{4}$ $\frac{4}{4}$ $\frac{5}{4}$

The number on the top indicates the number of beats in each measure.
The 4 on the bottom means that a ♩ = 1 beat.

Ex.

3 beats per measure
and ♩ = 1 beat

5 beats per measure
and ♩ = 1 beat

Explain the $\frac{5}{4}$ time signature for this piece.

5 means _____

4 means _____

Place a check next to the correct answers below.

In measure 1, the meaning of the word *molto* is:

_____ more

_____ much

The name of the last note in measure 4 is:

_____ F

_____ F♯

FJH2100

Place a check next to the correct answers below.

In measure 1, the curved line in the L.H. is a:

_____ tie

_____ slur

It means to:

_____ play *legato*

_____ hold the finger down for both note values

Improvisation

1. Play the L.H. notes as given.
2. Improvise in the R.H., using the five-finger patterns given.
3. Notice the time signature!
4. Repeat and play the R.H. one octave higher.
5. Give it a title.

_____

(Your title)

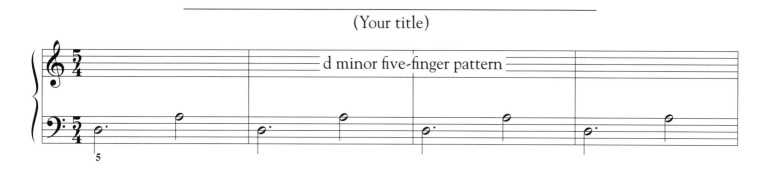

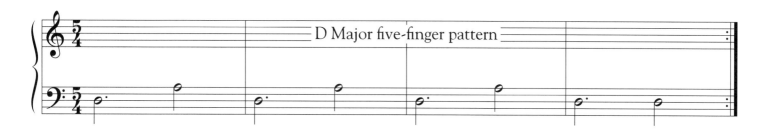

HERCULES' DANCE

from *Het derde musyck boexken . . . alderhande danserye*

attributed to Tielman Susato
(c. 1510–c. 1570)

Spotlight on Note Values

A dotted quarter note (♩.) = 1½ beats

An 8th note (♪) = ½ beat

Count it like this: ♩.   ♪

                      1   +   *2*   +

Write the counting in between the staffs for the first two measures.

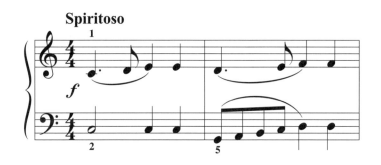

Place a check next to the correct answer below.

There are three dynamic markings in the composition: ***f***, ***mf***, and ⟨ . What do they mean?

_____ loud, medium loud, gradually softer

_____ loud, medium loud, gradually louder

Place a check next to the correct answers below.

Name the notes used in measures 5 and 6:

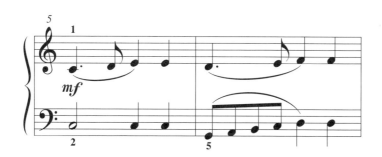

_____ dotted quarter, half, and quarter notes

_____ half, 16th, and dotted quarter notes

Name the following for the first two lines.

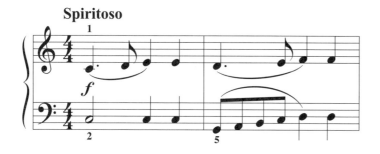

The R.H. five-finger pattern is:

_____ C Major

_____ G Major

The L.H. five-finger pattern is:

_____ C Major

_____ G Major

Skipping Dance
from *Nörmigers Tabulatur*

August Nörmiger
(c. 1560–c. 1613)
arr. Helen Marlais

Spotlight on Key Signatures

key signature — the sharps or flats next to the treble and bass clef at the beginning of a composition. The key signature indicates the name of the scale that was used to write the composition. The sharps or flats in the key signature must be played throughout the piece.

Naming key signatures

sharps — go up one half step from the last sharp.

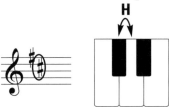

Key of D Major

flats — go to the next to the last.

Key of E♭ Major

Place a check next to the correct answers.

Name the key signature.

_____ F Major

_____ G Major

In measure 2, how many beats are there in the first three notes in the R.H.?

_____ 2

_____ 2½

The L.H. in the last two lines uses what two intervals? Place a check next to the correct answer.

_____ 4ths and 3rds

_____ 5ths and 4ths

Composition

1. Using any of these note values — ♩., ♪, ♫, ♩, or 𝅗𝅥 — write an ending to this 4-measure phrase.
2. Use the G Major five-finger pattern.
3. Write the counting in between the staffs.
4. When you are finished, play it to make sure you like it.
5. Give it a title.

_____
(Your title)

FJH2100

Baroque Era (c. 1600–c. 1750)

16

THE STATUES ARE DANCING

André Cardinal Destouches
(1672–1749)

Spotlight on Tonic and Dominant

tonic — the name of the first tone (degree) of a scale.

tonic

tonic triad — a triad whose lower note is the first degree of a scale.

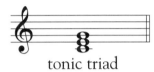

tonic triad

dominant — the name of the fifth tone (degree) of a scale.

dominant

dominant triad — a triad whose lower note is the fifth degree of a scale.

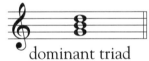

dominant triad

In measures 1-5, the L.H. uses only the tonic and the dominant of the C Major scale.
How many times is the dominant played? Place a check next to the correct answer.

_____ six times

_____ one time

In measures 6-11, the L.H. uses only the tonic and dominant of the C Major scale. How many times is the tonic played? Place a check next to the correct answer.

_____ seven times

_____ two times

The R.H. uses mostly notes from the tonic triad.

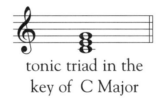

tonic triad in the
key of C Major

A note that passes in between two notes of a triad is called a passing tone.

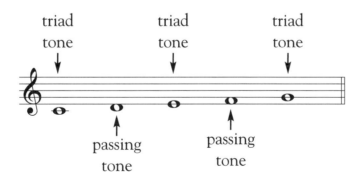

In the excerpt below, circle the notes that do **not** belong to the tonic triad.
Label them with a PT (passing tone).

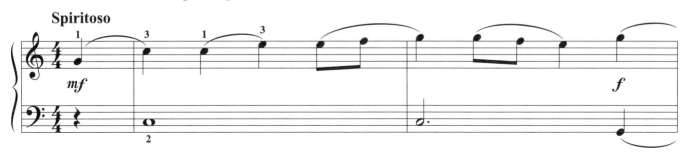

TWO BAROQUE MUSICIANS
from *Dictionaire de musique*

attributed to Sébastien de Brossard
(1655–1730)

Spotlight on the Major Scale

scale — eight notes in consecutive steps. It is named after the lowest note.

Major scale — all whole steps, except there is a half step between the third and fourth, and seventh and eighth notes.

Bb Major Scale

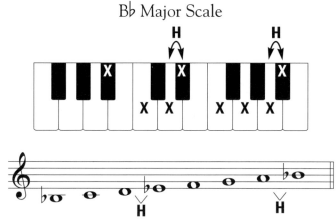

In the excerpt below, the notes of a descending Major scale are circled.
What is the name of this scale? Place a check next to the correct answer.

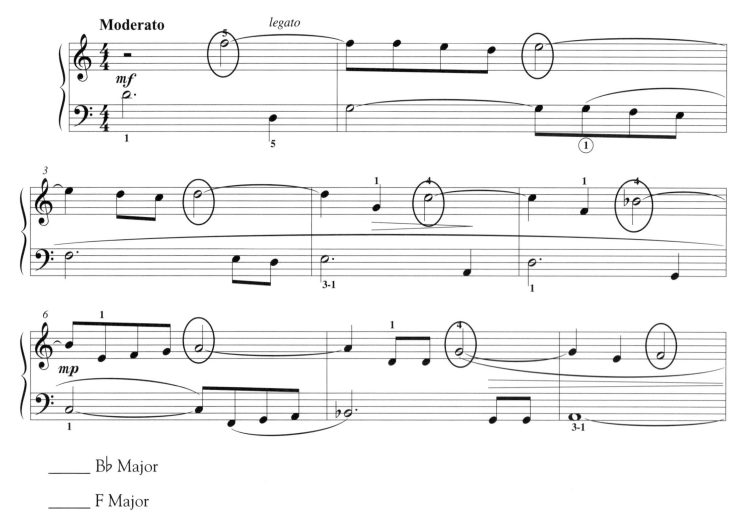

_____ Bb Major

_____ F Major

Place a check next to the correct answers below.

In the excerpt from the previous question, three pairs of measures have the same rhythm.
Which measures are they?

_____ Measures 2 and 6, 3 and 7, 1 and 8

_____ Measures 3 and 7, 2 and 6, 4 and 5

In the excerpt below:

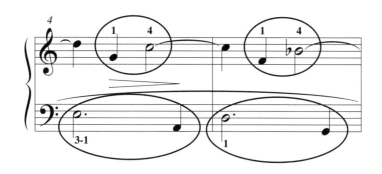

The circled notes in the R.H. are:

_____ 4ths

_____ 3rds

The circled notes in the L.H. are:

_____ 4ths

_____ 5ths

Improvisation

Using the d minor five-finger pattern, improvise a piece in which the L.H. **sometimes** imitates
(copies) the R.H., using the same notes and rhythm. Here's an example to get you started.

MINUET
Maaghdalena Dakkert
(fl. 1716)

Spotlight on Triads

triad — the first, third, and fifth notes of a five-finger pattern. It is named after the lowest note.

Major triad — the first, third, and fifth notes of a Major five-finger pattern.

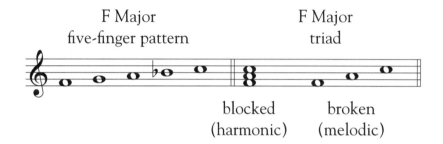

minor triad — the first, third, and fifth notes of a minor five-finger pattern.

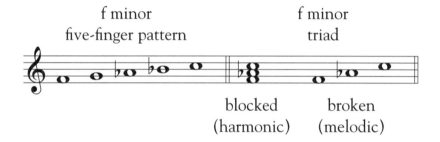

Place a check next to the correct answers below.

In measure 1, what is the name of the broken triad in the R.H.?

_____ A Major

_____ D Major

In measure 15, what is the name of the broken triad in the R.H.?

_____ A Major

_____ D Major

FJH2100

Place a check next to the correct answers below.

What is the name of the key signature?

_____ $\frac{3}{4}$

_____ D Major

What is the name of the time signature?

_____ $\frac{3}{4}$

_____ D Major

In measure 1, the L.H. begins on the:

_____ tonic

_____ dominant

In measures 13-16, circle the note in the L.H. that is **not** the tonic or dominant.

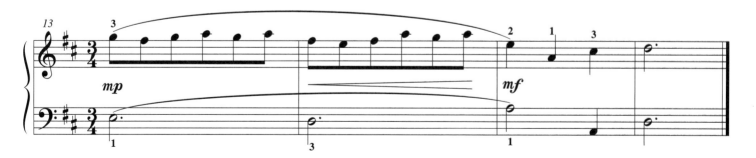

Bourrée

Maaghdalena Dakkert
(fl. 1716)

Spotlight on Dynamics

dynamics — the signs that indicate how soft or loud to play, such as f or p.

Place a check next to the correct answer below.

What is the meaning of the dynamics in the following measures?

Upbeat to measure 1:

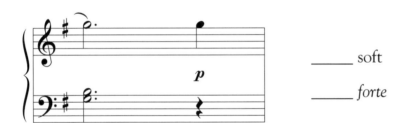

_____ medium fast

_____ medium loud

Measure 4:

_____ soft

_____ *forte*

Measure 6:

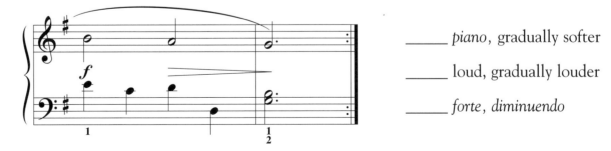

_____ gradually softer

_____ gradually louder

Measures 14 and 15:

_____ *piano*, gradually softer

_____ loud, gradually louder

_____ *forte, diminuendo*

Place a check next to the correct answers below.

Name the L.H. interval in measures 1, 2, and 3.

_____ 3rd

_____ 2nd

The R.H. note in the last measure is the:

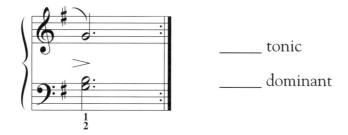

_____ tonic

_____ dominant

Composition

1. Finish this four-measure phrase, using blocked 3rds in the R.H.
2. Play and make sure you like it.
3. Write the counting in between the staffs.
4. Give it a title.

_____
(Your title)

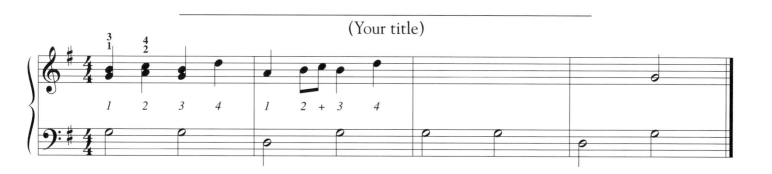

MINUET
from *Pieces de Viole, 1er Livre*

Marin Marais
(1656–1728)
arr. Helen Marlais

Spotlight on Motive

motive — a distinctive **rhythm, melody,** or **harmony,** or any combination of these,
that serves as a building block for a composition. It is most often found at the beginning,
appearing many times throughout.

Here is an example of a famous motive that appears at the beginning of Beethoven's *Fifth Symphony*.

The rhythm of the R.H. motive in measure 1 is found how many times in measures 9–14? _____

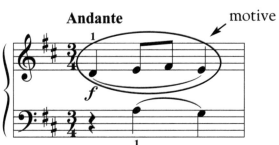

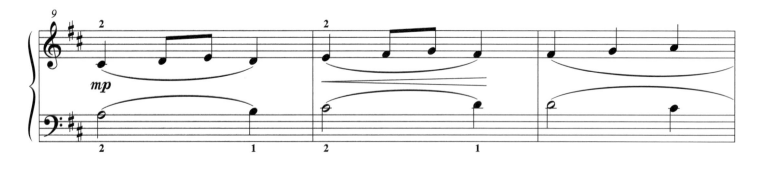

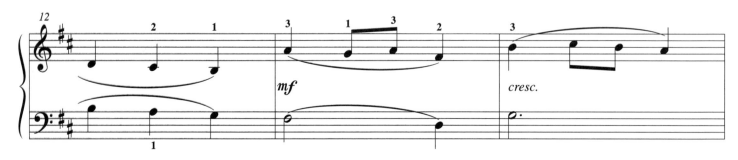

FJH2100

Name the key signature.

_____ Major

Place a check next to the correct answers below.

The L.H. notes in measure 2 are:

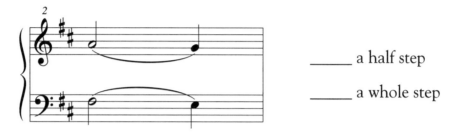

_____ a half step

_____ a whole step

The name for the dynamic marking in measure 10 is:

_____ *diminuendo*

_____ *crescendo*

The name of the L.H. triad in the last measure is:

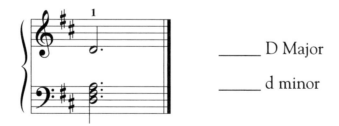

_____ D Major

_____ d minor

This triad in the last measure is the:

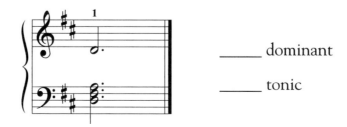

_____ dominant

_____ tonic

FJH2100

NOËL
(Do You Know My Dear Neighbor?)

arr. Jean-François Dandrieu
(c. 1682–1738)

Spotlight on Accidentals

accidental — a sharp (♯), flat (♭), or natural (♮) placed before a note.

Put a check next to the correct answers below.

The accidental in measure 5 is a:

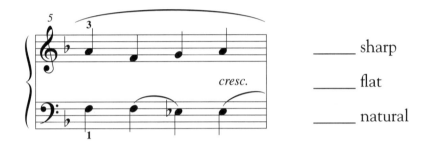

_____ sharp

_____ flat

_____ natural

The accidental in measure 6 is a:

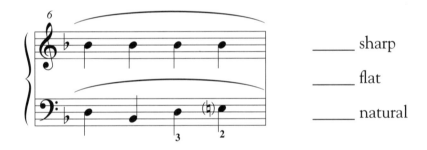

_____ sharp

_____ flat

_____ natural

The *Allegretto* tempo marking means:

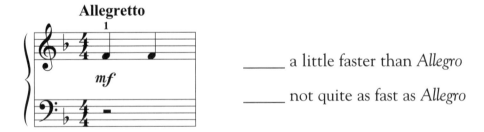

_____ a little faster than *Allegro*

_____ not quite as fast as *Allegro*

The key signature of this piece is:

_____ 4/4

_____ F Major

Place a check next to the correct answers below.

In measure 11, the L.H. note on the 4th beat is the:

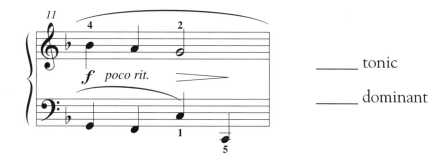

_____ tonic

_____ dominant

In the last measure, the notes in the R.H. and L.H. are the:

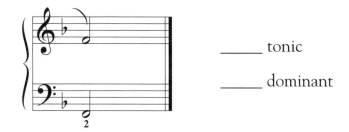

_____ tonic

_____ dominant

In measure 11, *poco* means:

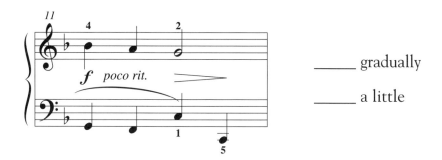

_____ gradually

_____ a little

Improvisation

1. R.H. — use any notes from the F Major scale.
2. Start with the notes below.
3. Notice the fingering at the beginning.
4. Keep going and have fun!

Classical Era (c. 1750–c. 1820)

Scherzo

from *The First Lessons for the Harpsichord or Spinnet*

Johann Andreas Kauchlitz Colizzi
(c. 1740–c. 1790)
arr. Helen Marlais

Spotlight on Binary Form

form — the plan of construction of a composition that exists in the mind of the composer. The structure of a composition.

binary (2-part) form — called AA^1 or AB form. It consists of two sections. The first section ends on the **dominant** and the second section ends on the **tonic.** Often the sections begin alike.

Place a check next to the correct answers below.

In measure 4, the last note in the L.H. is:

_____ the tonic

_____ the dominant

In the last measure, the last note in the L.H. is:

_____ the tonic

_____ the dominant

This composition uses the binary form.

_____ True

_____ False

THE BOHEMIAN

from *The First Lessons for the Harpsichord or Spinnet*

Johann Andreas Kauchlitz Colizzi
(c. 1740–c. 1790)
arr. Helen Marlais

Spotlight on Rests

whole rest	half rest	quarter rest	eighth rest
the whole measure	2 beats	1 beat	½ beat
(3 or 4 beats)			

rest — a sign of silence.

Place a check next to the correct answers below.

In measures 3 and 4 there are some rests. They are called:

_____ whole rest, eighth rest

_____ half rest, quarter rest

_____ half rest, eighth rest

This piece is written in the key of:

_____ A Major

_____ D Major

In measure 4, the last note in the L.H. is A. It is the:

_____ tonic

_____ dominant

In measure 8, the last note in the L.H. is D. It is the:

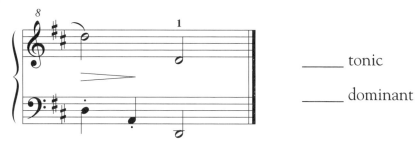

_____ tonic

_____ dominant

What is the name of the form that the composer used for this piece?

_____ binary

_____ ternary

FJH2100

THE SCALE LADDER
Daniel Gottlob Türk
(1750–1813)

Spotlight on the Major Scale

scale — eight notes in consecutive steps. It is named after the lowest note.

major scale — all whole steps, except there is a half step between the third and fourth, and the seventh and eighth notes.

A Major Scale

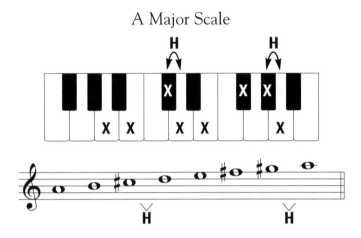

Place a check next to the correct answers below.

The first eight notes in the R.H. form what Major scale?

_____ Major

The circled interval in measures 3 and 4 are:

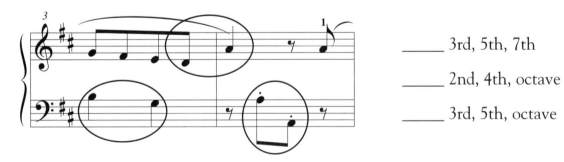

_____ 3rd, 5th, 7th

_____ 2nd, 4th, octave

_____ 3rd, 5th, octave

The tempo marking *Allegro non troppo* means:

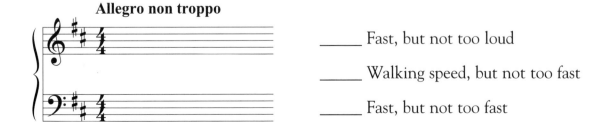

_____ Fast, but not too loud

_____ Walking speed, but not too fast

_____ Fast, but not too fast

Softly, Like the Wind

Daniel Gottlob Türk
(1750–1813)

Spotlight on Key Signatures

key signature — the sharps or flats next to the treble and bass clef at the beginning of a composition. The key signature indicates the name of the scale that was used to write the composition. The sharps or flats in the key signature must be played throughout the piece.

Naming key signatures

sharps — go up one half step from the last sharp.

Key of D Major

The last **sharp** is C♯.
Up one half step
from C♯ is D.

flats — go to the next to the last flat.

Key of E♭ Major

The next to last **flat** is E♭.
This is the name of the key.

Softly, Like the Wind is written in the key of:

 _____ Major

Composition

This composition is in binary form.

1. Finish the R.H. in measures 3, 4, 7, and 8.
2. Play your composition to make sure you like it.
3. Write the counting in between the staffs.
4. Give it a title!

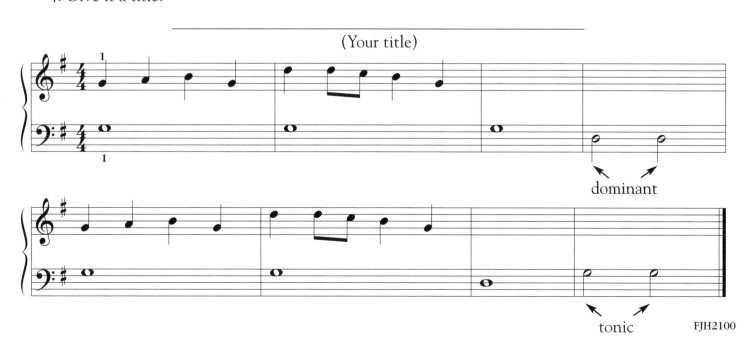

(Your title)

dominant

tonic

FJH2100

A Little Waltz

Daniel Gottlob Türk
(1750–1813)

Spotlight on the Major Triad

Major triad — the first, third, and fifth notes of a **Major five-finger pattern.**
It is named after the **lowest** note.

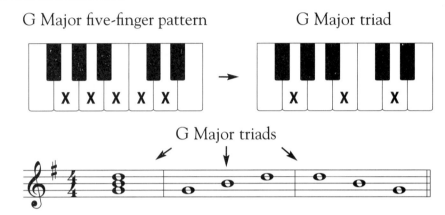

Place a check next to the correct answers below.

The circled notes in measures 1 and 2 form what Major triad?

_____ D Major

_____ A Major

The circled triad above is the:

_____ tonic

_____ dominant

The key signature shows that we are in what Major key?

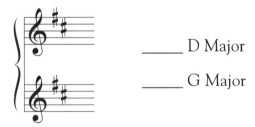

_____ D Major

_____ G Major

What two types of articulation are found in measures 4 and 5?

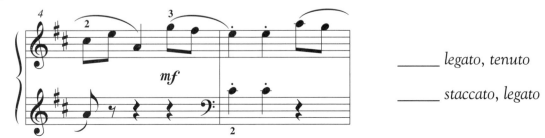

_____ *legato, tenuto*

_____ *staccato, legato*

FJH2100

PRELUDE
from *A Set of Progressive Lessons for the Harpsichord or the Piano Forte*

Samuel Arnold
(1740–1802)

Spotlight on Tempo

tempo — the speed at which a composition is played. Some examples are:

Adagio — slow
Allegro — fast and cheerful
Andante — walking speed
Andantino — slightly faster than *Andante*

Moderato — moderate speed
Largo — very slow
Larghetto — not quite as slow as *Largo*

Place a check next to the correct answers below.

What is the tempo of this piece?

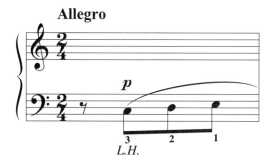

____ $\frac{2}{4}$

____ fast and cheerful

____ C Major

What is the time signature of this piece?

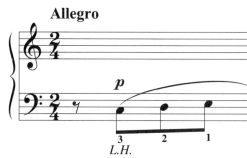

____ $\frac{2}{4}$

____ fast and cheerful

____ C Major

In measure 3, the words *sempre crescendo* mean

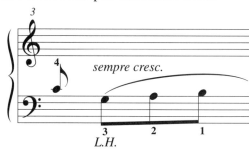

____ always *crescendo*

____ a little *crescendo*

What is the name of the Major scale formed by the last eight notes?

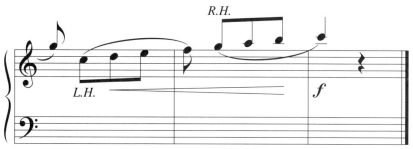

____ G Major

____ C Major

34

ALLEGRETTO
from *24 Short and Easy Pieces, Opus 1*

Alexander Reinagle
(1756–1809)

Spotlight on *-etto* and *-ino*

-etto and *-ino* — commonly added onto the end of tempo markings. They both mean "little."
For example, *Larghetto* means a little *Largo,* not as slow as *Largo.*

Place a check next to the correct answers below.

The title of this piece indicates the tempo. What does *Allegretto* mean?

_____ a little fast, not as fast as *Allegro*

_____ a little slow, not as slow as *Allegro*

This piece is in the key of:

_____ F Major

_____ G Major

The dynamics used in measures 1, 4, and 5 include $\boldsymbol{p}$, $\diagdown$, and $\boldsymbol{f}$. What do they mean?

_____ soft, gradually louder, and loud

_____ soft, gradually softer, and loud

The last L.H. note in the last measure is the:

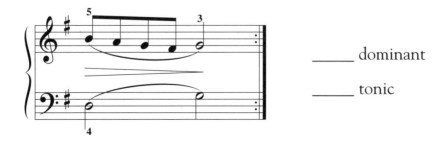

_____ dominant

_____ tonic

FJH2100

CHILDREN'S SONG
Daniel Gottlob Türk
(1750–1813)

Spotlight on Articulation

articulation — the degree to which the notes are separated or connected, such as **legato** or **staccato.** See the *Glossary of Musical Terms* (starting on page 68) for other types of articulation.

Place a check next to the correct answers below.

In measures 7 and 8, there are three types of articulation. What are they?

_____ *legato, tenuto, staccato*

_____ *tenuto, portato, legato*

In measures 1-4, the L.H. uses what Major five-finger pattern?

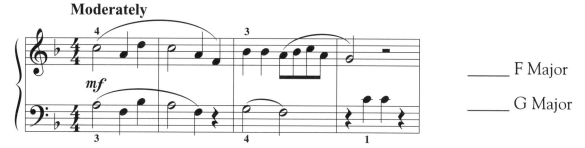

_____ F Major

_____ G Major

Improvisation

1. Play the L.H. notes as given.
2. Improvise in the R.H., using the given five-finger patterns.
3. Use both *legato* and *staccato* in the R.H.
4. Make up your own special ending after the 8th measure, if you wish.
5. Play it for your teacher at your next lesson.

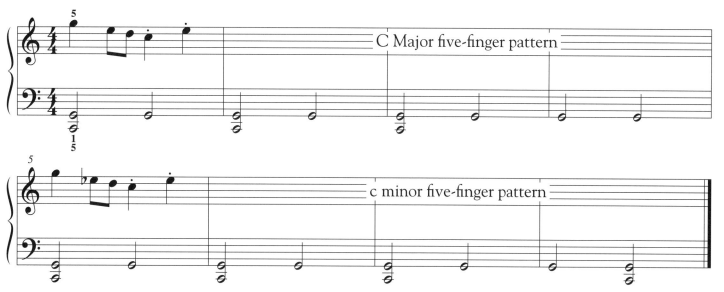

ALLEGRO
from *24 Short and Easy Pieces, Opus 1*

Alexander Reinagle
(1756–1809)

Spotlight on Major and Minor Five-Finger Patterns

Major five-finger pattern — all whole steps except there is a half step
between the third and fourth keys. It is named after the **lowest** note.

F Major five-finger pattern

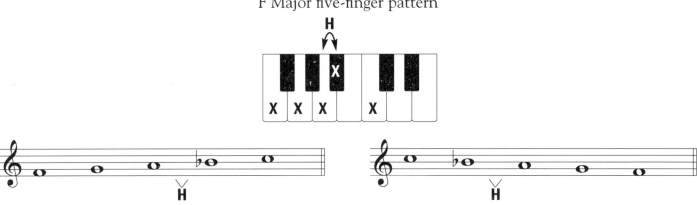

minor five-finger pattern — all whole steps except there is a half step
between the second and third keys. It is named after the **lowest** note.

f minor five-finger pattern

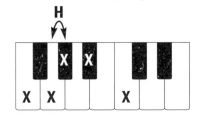

Place a check next to the correct answer below.

In measures 1-4, put your fingers over all the notes in the R.H.
What is the name of the five-finger pattern?

_____ C Major

_____ G Major

FJH2100

Place a check next to the correct answers below.

The R.H. uses the same five-finger pattern throughout the composition, except for one measure.
In measures 9-12, which measure goes out of the five-finger pattern you named in the previous question.

_____ measure 10

_____ measure 11

The L.H. uses only one five-finger pattern throughout the entire piece.
Look at the first four measures below. The name of this five-finger pattern is:

_____ E Major

_____ C Major

Look at the L.H. notes from the previous question. This same pattern of intervals is used throughout the entire piece, except for the third line. What are the names of the intervals above?

_____ 3rds, 2nds, and 4ths

_____ 3rds, 2nds, and 5ths

The title of this piece, *Allegro*, indicates a tempo. What should it be?

_____ Walking speed, moderately slow

_____ Fast and cheerful

SUNSET AT THE BOARDWALK

from *First Instruction in Piano-Playing:*
One Hundred Recreations

Carl Czerny
(1791–1857)

Spotlight on Intervals

interval — the distance between two keys on the staff or keyboard.

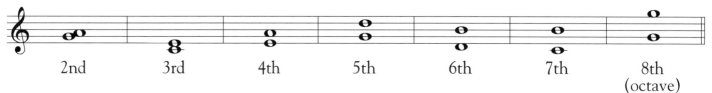

Place a check next to the correct answers below.

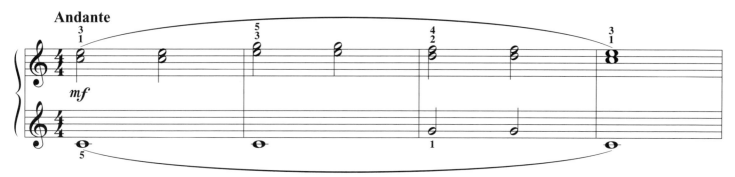

What is the name of the interval played by the R.H. in the first line?

_____ 2nd

_____ 3rd

_____ 4th

Both hands play in the same clef. What is the name of it?

_____ treble clef

_____ bass clef

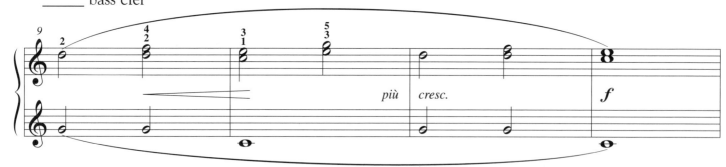

There are three dynamic markings in the third line. What do they mean?

_____ gradually louder, a little *crescendo*, soft

_____ gradually softer, more *crescendo*, loud

_____ gradually louder, more *crescendo*, loud

_____ gradually louder, less *crescendo*, loud

FJH2100

Place a check next to the correct answers below.

In the L.H., how many times does the composer use the tonic in the first four measures?

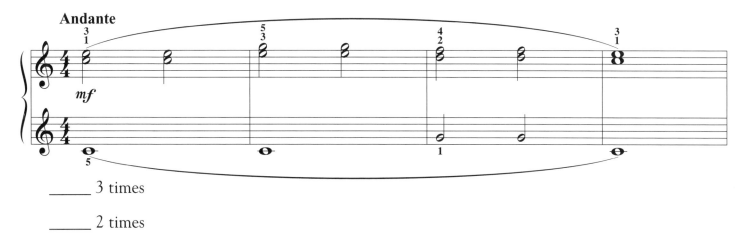

_____ 3 times

_____ 2 times

What is the meaning of the tempo marking?

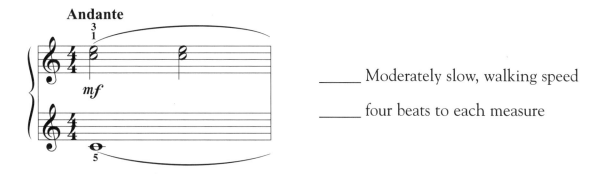

_____ Moderately slow, walking speed

_____ four beats to each measure

Composition

1. Finish measures 3-4 and 7-8 of this composition. Notice that both hands use the treble clef.
2. Play your composition to make sure you like it.
3. Write the counting under the notes.
4. Give it a title.

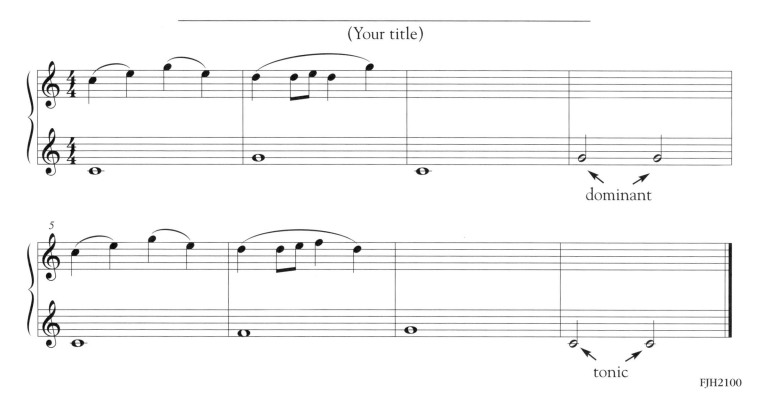

MONDAY MARCH
from *First Instruction in Piano-Playing:*
One Hundred Recreations

Carl Czerny
(1791–1857)

Spotlight on Triads

triad — the first, third, and fifth notes of a **five-finger pattern.** It is named after lowest note.

Major triad — the first, third, and fifth notes of a **Major five-finger** pattern.

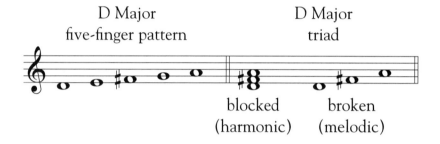

minor triad — the first, third, and fifth notes of a **minor five-finger pattern.**

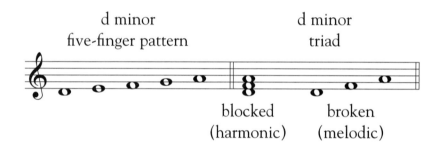

Place a check next to the correct answers below.

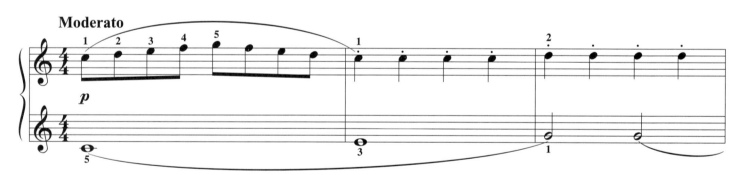

In the first line, the composer uses a broken triad in the L.H. What is the name of the triad?

_____ C Major

_____ G Major

The L.H. triad in the previous question is called the:

_____ tonic

_____ dominant

Place a check next to the correct answers below.

The composer uses only one five-finger pattern throughout the composition.
Look at measures 7-9 below:

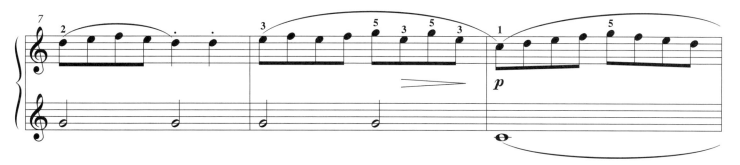

The five-finger pattern is:

_____ D Major

_____ C Major

How many times is the tonic played in the L.H.?

_____ one time

_____ four times

In measures 10-12, which measure has two types of articulation?

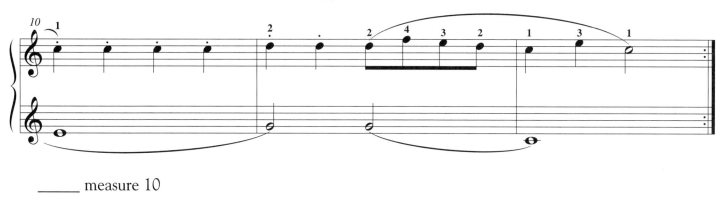

_____ measure 10

_____ measure 11

_____ measure 12

What is the meaning of the tempo marking?

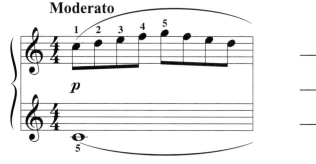

_____ softly

_____ play at a medium speed

_____ four beats per measure

THE COBBLESTONE ROAD
from *24 Short and Easy Pieces, Opus 1*

Alexander Reinagle
(1756–1809)

Spotlight on Motive

motive — a distinctive **rhythm, melody,** or **harmony,** or any combination of these,
that serves as a building block for a composition. It is most often found at the beginning,
appearing many times throughout.

Here is an example of a famous **motive** that appears at the beginning of Beethoven's *Fifth Symphony*.

Place a check next to the correct answers below.

The motive for this composition is seen in measure 1.
It consists of the notes from what Major triad?

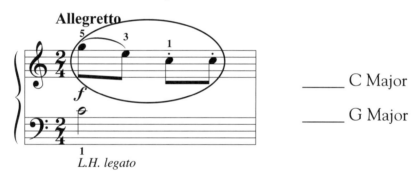

_____ C Major

_____ G Major

The triad from the previous question is the:

_____ tonic

_____ dominant

In measures 9-11 both the rhythm and the articulations of the motive are repeated,
but this time the composer uses what Major triad?

_____ D Major

_____ G Major

Place a check next to the correct answers below.

The broken triads from measures 9 and 11 in the previous question are the:

_____ tonic

_____ dominant

What are the two types of articulations used in the motive?

_____ *staccato, portato*

_____ *legato, portato*

_____ *legato, staccato*

What type of articulation is used in the last measure?

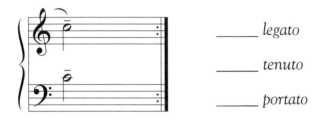

_____ *legato*

_____ *tenuto*

_____ *portato*

Improvisation

1. Make up a piece that uses both *staccato* and *legato*.
2. Use the given L.H. and R.H.
3. Play an octave higher in the second line.
4. Keep going and make up your own special ending.

F Major five-finger pattern

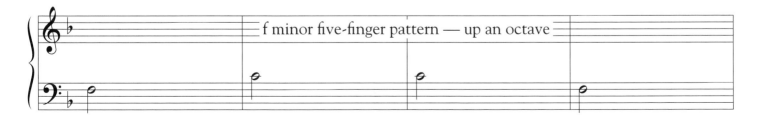

f minor five-finger pattern — up an octave

Romantic Era (c. 1820–c. 1900)

SOLDIER'S SONG
Moritz Vogel
(1846–1922)

Spotlight on Dynamics

dynamics — the signs that indicate how soft or loud to play, such as f or p.

The composer has indicated dynamics in measures 5, 6, 7, 10, and 11.
Give the name and meaning of each dynamic.

name (***mf***) _____

meaning _____

name (◁) _____

meaning _____

name (▷) _____

meaning _____

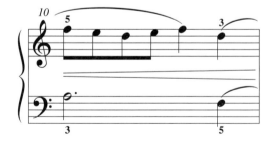

name (***mp***) _____

meaning _____

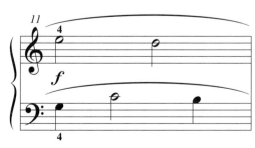

name (◁) _____

meaning _____

name (***f***) _____

meaning _____

FJH2100

Mark the intervals in the L.H. in measures 1 and 2. The first one is done for you.

2nd ___ ___ ___ ___ ___

Mark the intervals in the R.H. in measures 3 and 4. The first one is done for you.

2nd ___ ___ ___ ___ ___

Are the above intervals in the R.H. and L.H. the same or different? Check one.

_____ same

_____ different

Compare measures 5 and 6 with measures 7 and 8 below.

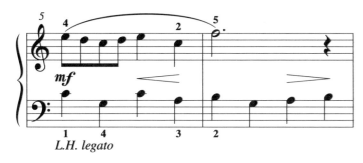 

What is the same about them? Check **three**.

_____ intervals

_____ rhythm

_____ dynamics

_____ articulation

What is different about them? Check **one**.

_____ intervals

_____ rhythm

_____ dynamics

_____ articulation

IN THE GARDEN

from *Children's Album, Opus 210*

Louis Köhler
(1820–1886)

Spotlight on Tonic and Dominant

tonic — the first degree (note) of a **scale.** Also, a **triad** built on the first degree of a scale.

dominant — the fifth degree (note) of a **scale.** Also, a **triad** built on the fifth degree of a scale.

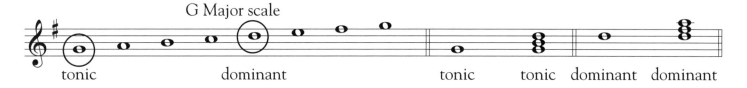

Place a check next to the correct answers below.

According to the key signature, this composition is written in the key of:

_____ F Major

_____ B♭ Major

In measure 15, the circled note is the:

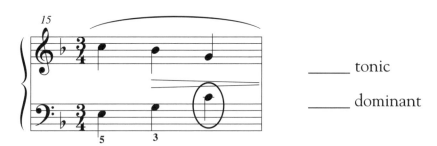

_____ tonic

_____ dominant

In measure 16, the circled note is the:

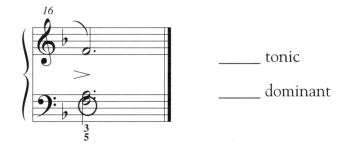

_____ tonic

_____ dominant

Place a check next to the correct answers below.

What is the meaning of the tempo marking?

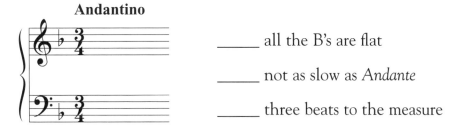

_____ all the B's are flat

_____ not as slow as *Andante*

_____ three beats to the measure

In measures 9 and 10, the notes in both the R.H. and the L.H. belong to what triad?

_____ F Major

_____ A Major

In measures 13 and 14, the notes in both the R.H. and the L.H. belong to what triad?

_____ C Major

_____ F Major

Composition

1. Finish the R.H. in measures 3-8.
2. Use any notes from the D Major five-finger pattern.
3. Play your composition to make sure you like it.
4. Write the counting in between the staffs.
5. Give it a title.

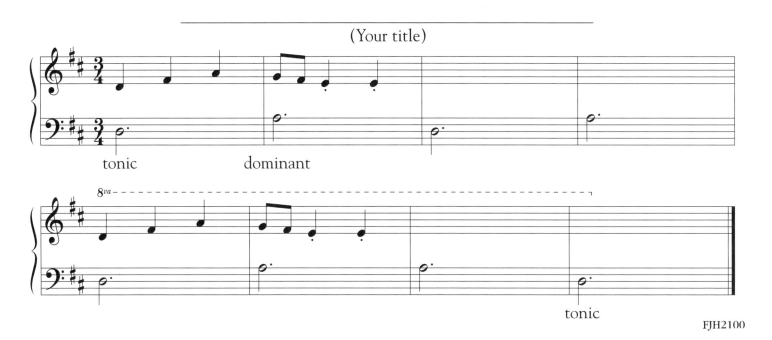

(Your title)

tonic   dominant

tonic

FJH2100

GOING TO SCHOOL
(Opus 117, No. 14)

Cornelius Gurlitt
(1820–1901)

Spotlight on Key Signatures

key signature — the sharps or flats next to the treble and bass clef at the beginning of a composition. The key signature indicates the name of the scale that was used to write the composition.

Naming key signatures

sharps — go up one half step
from the last sharp.

flats — go to the next
to the last flat.

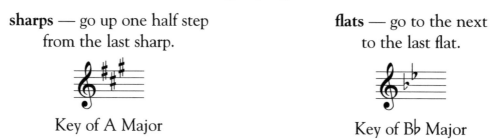

Key of A Major   Key of B♭ Major

Place a check next to the correct answers below.

According to the key signature, this composition is in the key of:

_____ G Major

_____ F♯ Major

In measures 1 and 2, what is the name of the five-finger pattern in the R.H.?

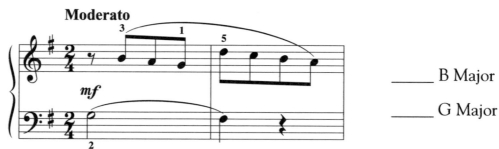

Moderato

mf

_____ B Major

_____ G Major

See measure 1 in the previous question. What is the name of the rest in the R.H.?
How many beats does it receive?

_____ quarter rest — 1 beat

_____ eighth rest — 1 beat

_____ eighth rest — ½ beat

_____ quarter rest — ½ beat

Place a check next to the correct answers below.

In measure 8, which is halfway through the piece, the note in the L.H. is the:

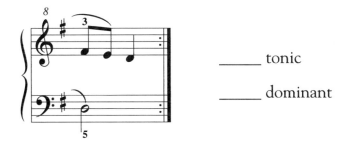

_____ tonic

_____ dominant

In measure 16, the last measure of the piece, the note in the L.H. is the:

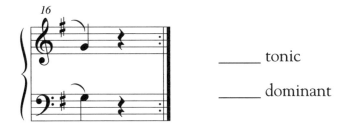

_____ tonic

_____ dominant

Based on the answers from the two previous questions, what is the form of this piece?

_____ binary form

_____ ternary form

The motive of this composition is circled below.
Circle the three places in the first 12 measures where the rhythm of the motive is repeated.

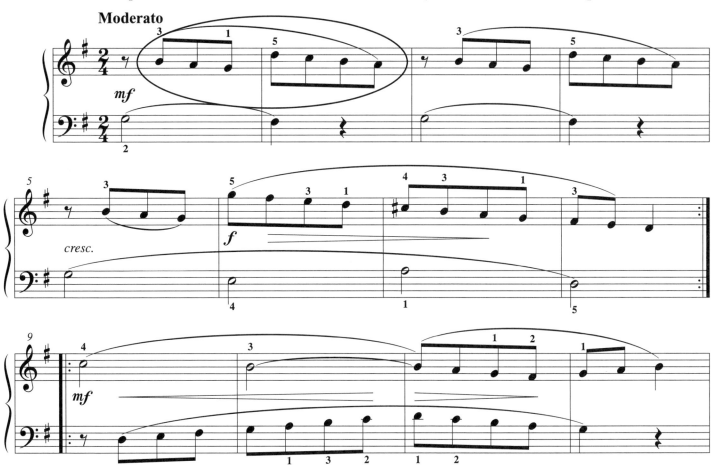

FJH2100

WATER SPRITE
from *Fifty Pieces Without Octaves,*
Opus 70, No. 27

Hermann Berens
(1826–1880)

Spotlight on Tempo

tempo — the speed at which a composition is played. The tempo marking is found in the upper left-hand corner at the beginning of a composition. See the *Glossary of Musical Terms* (starting on page 68) for a list.

Place a check next to the correct answers below.

The tempo of this piece means:

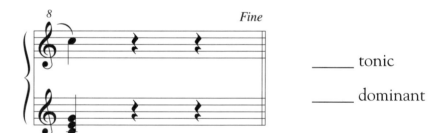

_____ play a little bit fast

_____ play very fast

_____ play fast

In measure 8, the circled L.H. triad is called the:

_____ tonic

_____ dominant

See measure 8 in the previous question. What is the meaning of the word *Fine?*

_____ go to the end

_____ the end

In measure 16, the circled triad is called the:

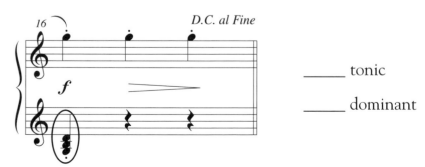

_____ tonic

_____ dominant

Place a check next to the correct answers below.

See measure 16 in the previous question. What is the meaning of *D.C. al Fine?*

_____ go to the sign and play to the *Fine*

_____ go back to the beginning and play to the *Fine*

The motive of this composition is circled in measure 1. Including the motive,
how many times is the rhythm of the motive found in the first two lines?

_____ four times

_____ six times

Improvisation

Follow these guidelines. The first measure is given.

1. Use any notes from the G Major scale in the R.H.
2. Repeat the L.H. notes throughout the entire piece.
3. Experiment with different dynamics. Experiment playing in different octaves.
4. End on the given notes or any other way you like.

or end another way if you like

HAPPILY EXERCISING

Ferdinand Beyer
(1803–1863)

Spotlight on Ternary Form

ternary form — consists of three parts. This form is often referred to as ABA form or three-part form.
The first and last parts are alike and are called A. If the last part is slightly different than
the first part, it is called A¹. The middle part is different than the A parts and is called B.

This composition is in ternary (three-part) form. The first three lines are shown below.
There are two more lines after the third line that are not shown.
Does the B section begin on the second or third line? Place a check next to the correct answer below.

_____ second line

_____ third line

Place a check next to the correct answers below.

The last two measures of the first and last section are shown below.
In ternary form what are these sections called?

Last two measures of the first section:

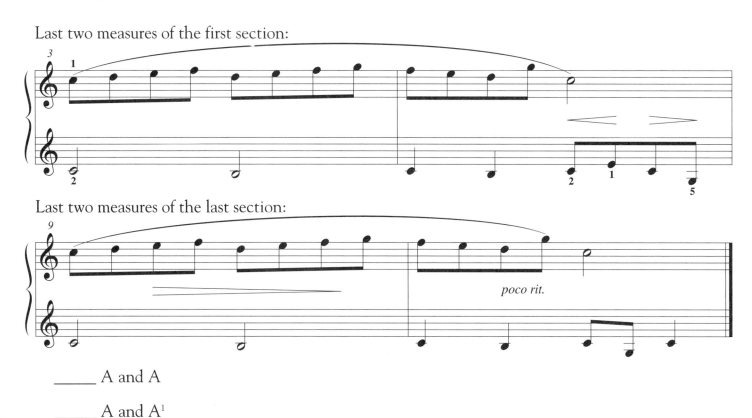

Last two measures of the last section:

_____ A and A

_____ A and A¹

How many slurs are in the first two lines?

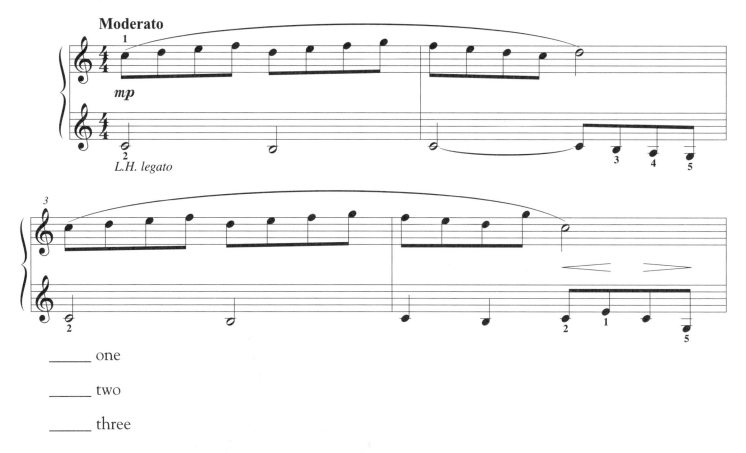

_____ one

_____ two

_____ three

THE MIGHTY HAWK
(Opus 117, No. 8)

Cornelius Gurlitt
(1820–1901)

Spotlight on Motive

motive — a distinctive **rhythm, melody,** or **harmony,** or any combination of these,
that serves as a building block for a composition. It is most often found at the beginning,
appearing many times throughout.

The motive in this composition is circled in measure 1 below.
In the first two lines, circle the other places where the motive is found.

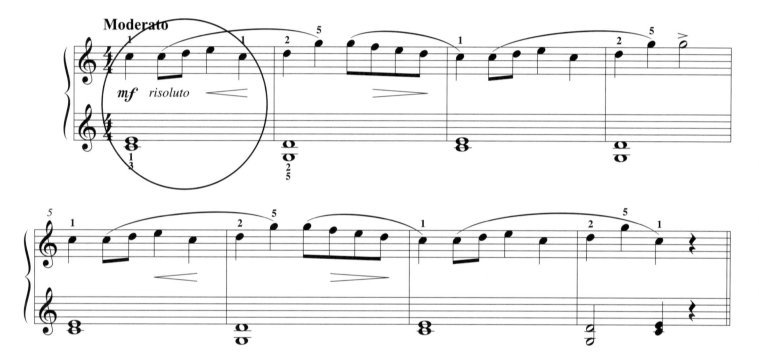

Place a check next to the correct answers below.

In measure 1 of the music above, what is the meaning of *risoluto?*

_____ remember to *crescendo*

_____ boldly, vigorously, decisively

In measure 1 of the music above, what is the name of the interval in the L.H.?

_____ 2nd

_____ 3rd

FJH2100

Place a check next to the correct answers below.

What is the letter name of the circled note in measure 2?

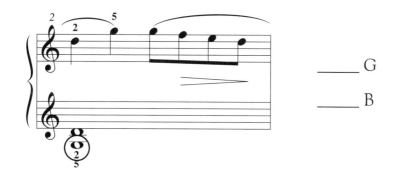

_____ G

_____ B

In measure 2 above, the circled note is the:

_____ tonic

_____ dominant

Composition

1. The motive in this composition is circled in measures 1 and 2.
2. Complete measures 5, 6, and 7, using the rhythm of the motive once.
3. Write the counting under the notes.
4. Play your composition to make sure you like it.
5. Give it a title!

(Your title)

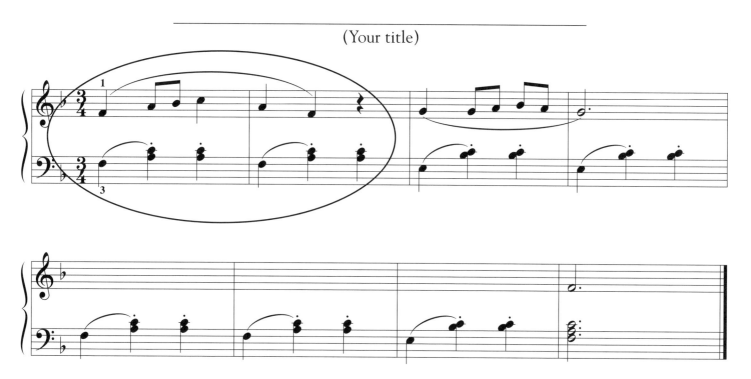

20TH/21ST CENTURIES (1900–PRESENT)

THE SPARROW'S SONG
Timothy Brown
(b. 1959)

Spotlight on Melody

melody — a pattern of notes and rhythms in a certain order. In piano music, the melody is different than the harmony, which is made up of chords. In order to tell which part has the melody, choose the part that is most likely singable.

Place a check next to the correct answers below.

In measures 1-4, which hand has the melody?

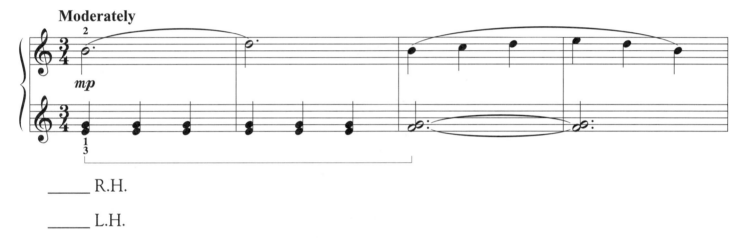

_____ R.H.

_____ L.H.

In measures 13 and 14, which hand has the melody?

_____ R.H.

_____ L.H.

In measures 15, 16, and 17, which hand has the melody?

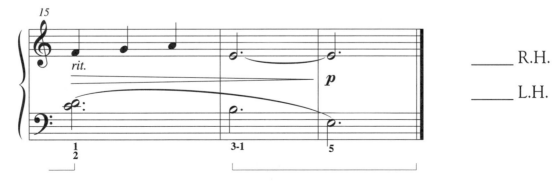

_____ R.H.

_____ L.H.

Place a check next to the correct answers below.

The sign that is circled under measures 1 and 2 means to:

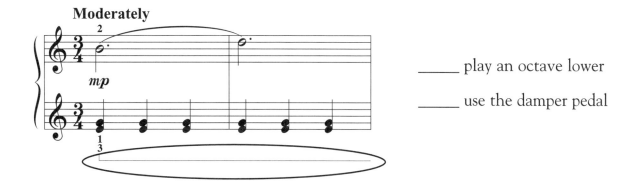

_____ play an octave lower

_____ use the damper pedal

Compare the first three measures in lines 1 and 2.

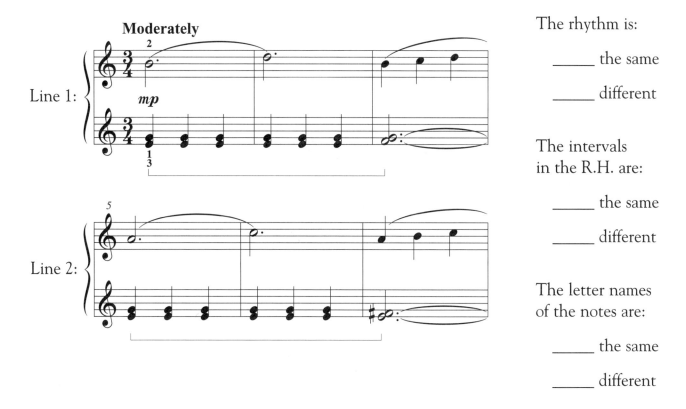

The rhythm is:

_____ the same

_____ different

The intervals
in the R.H. are:

_____ the same

_____ different

The letter names
of the notes are:

_____ the same

_____ different

The notes circled in measure 13 belong to what triad?

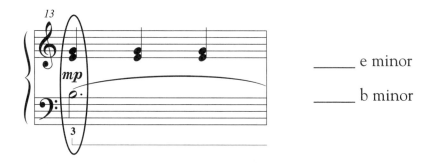

_____ e minor

_____ b minor

STUDY
from *The First Term at the Piano*

Béla Bartók
(1881–1945)

Spotlight on Major and Minor Five-Finger Patterns

Major five-finger pattern — all whole steps except there is a half step between the third and fourth keys. It is named after the **lowest** note.

E Major five-finger pattern

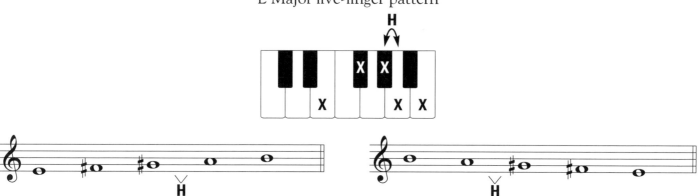

minor five-finger pattern — all whole steps except there is a half step between the second and third keys. It is named after the **lowest** note.

e minor five-finger pattern

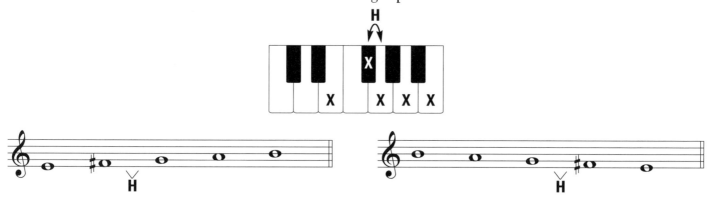

Place a check next to the correct answer below.

What is the name of the five-finger pattern that is circled in measures 2, 3, and 4?

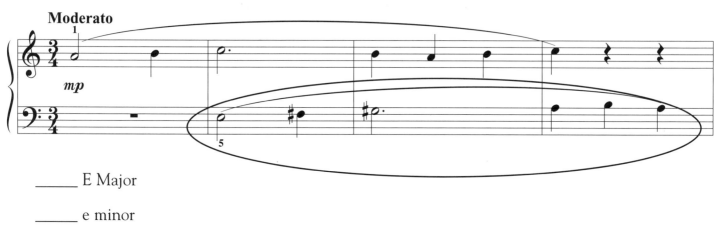

_____ E Major

_____ e minor

FJH2100

Place a check next to the correct answers below.

Circle the accidentals in measures 6 and 7.

The rests in measure 8 get how many beats each?

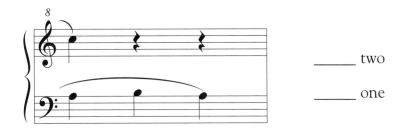

_____ two

_____ one

What is the name of the rest from the previous question?

_____ quarter rest

_____ eighth rest

Improvisation

1. Improvise, using the given L.H. notes and the f minor five-finger pattern.
2. Try using some f minor triads in your R.H.
3. Experiment playing in different octaves.
4. Use the damper pedal if desired.

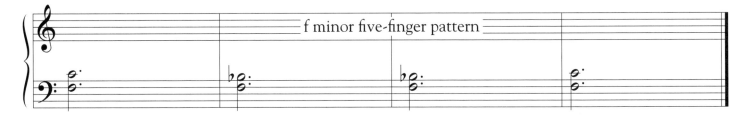

GRADUS NO. 8
from *Gradus: 40 Studies for Piano, Book 1*

Samuel Adler
(b. 1928)

Spotlight on Time Signatures

time signature — the numbers at the beginning of a piece.

The number on the top indicates the number of beats per measure.

The 4 on the bottom means that a ♩ gets 1 beat.

Answer the following questions about the music below. Place a check next to the correct answers.

Notice the changing time signatures in this composition. The first three measures have a distinctive rhythm that is the motive of this piece. How many times is this rhythm repeated, including the motive?

_____ four

_____ two

What is the name of the circled triad in measure 1?

_____ A Major

_____ a minor

The names of the two sharps in this piece are F♯ and C♯.
If there were a key signature with these two sharps, what would be the name of the key?

_____ D Major

_____ A Major

POLKA
from *Twenty-Four Little Pieces, Opus 39*

Dmitri Kabalevsky
(1904–1987)

Spotlight on Melody

melody — a pattern of notes and rhythms in a certain order. In piano music, the melody is different than the harmony, which is made up of chords. In order to tell which hand has the melody, choose the hand that is most likely to be singable.

Place a check next to the correct answers below.

In measures 1 and 2, which hand has the melody?

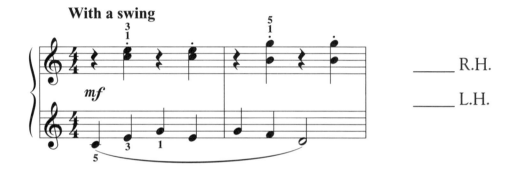

_____ R.H.

_____ L.H.

Name the circled interval in measure 3:

_____ 5th

_____ 6th

Name the circled triad in measure 4:

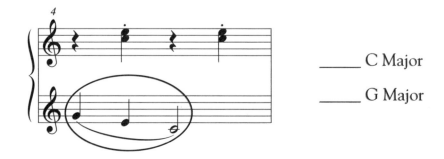

_____ C Major

_____ G Major

TIRESOME PRANK
No. 3 from Peccadilles importunes

Erik Satie
(1866–1925)

Spotlight on Metronome Markings

metronome marking — this marking is sometimes found next to the **tempo** marking at the top left of the first page. Two sample metronome markings are shown below.

♩ = 72   ♪ = ca. 60

The first metronome marking means there is one click per beat (♩) and the metronome is set at a speed of 72 beats per minute. The second marking means that there is one click per half beat (♪) and the metronome is set at a speed of approximately (ca.) 60 beats per minute.

Place a check next to the correct answers below.

What is the meaning of the metronome marking in this composition?

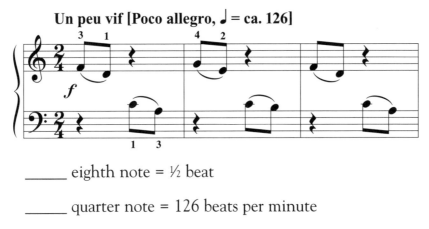

Un peu vif [Poco allegro, ♩ = ca. 126]

_____ eighth note = ½ beat

_____ quarter note = 126 beats per minute

_____ quarter note = approximately 126 beats per minute

The tempo marking in the music above means:

_____ a little fast

_____ fast

_____ very fast

The time signature means:

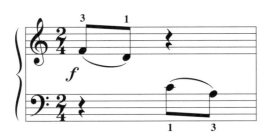

_____ there are two quarter notes in each measure and the quarter note gets one beat

_____ there are two beats in each measure and the quarter note gets one beat

Place a check next to the correct answers below.

The rest in measure 5 gets how many beats?

_____ 4 beats

_____ 2 beats

Write the names of the circled intervals in measures 17 and 18. For example, 2nd, 3rd, 4th, etc.

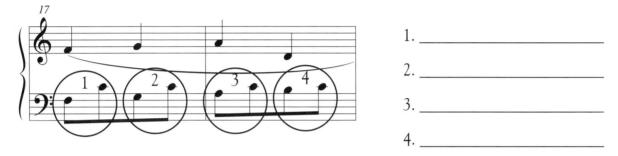

1. _____

2. _____

3. _____

4. _____

The [rit.] at the end of the piece means to:

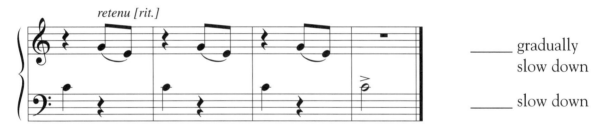

_____ gradually
slow down

_____ slow down

Composition

1. The motive is circled in the first two measures.
2. Complete the R.H. in measures 5 and 6, using the same rhythm as the motive.
3. Use the G Major five-finger pattern.
4. Write the counting under the notes and play your composition to make sure you like it.

PLAYING
from *Twenty-Four Little Pieces, Opus 39, No. 5*

Dmitri Kabalevsky
(1904–1987)

Spotlight on Intervals

interval — the distance between two keys on the piano or two notes on the staff.

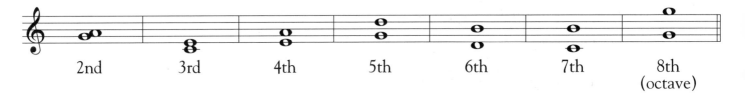

Name the circled intervals in measures 19, 20, and 21. For example, 2nd, 3rd, 4th, etc.

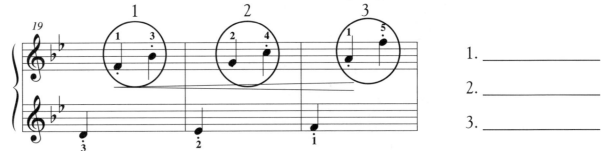

1. _____

2. _____

3. _____

Place a check next to the correct answers below.

According to the key signature, this piece is in the key of:

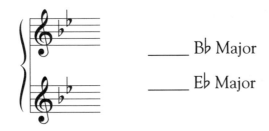

_____ B♭ Major

_____ E♭ Major

The L.H. in the last measure is the:

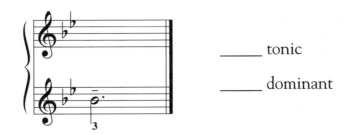

_____ tonic

_____ dominant

Place a check next to the correct answers below.

There are two types of articulation in the last two measures of this piece.
What are they? Check **two.**

_____ legato

_____ staccato

_____ tenuto

_____ portato

Label the whole (W) and half (H) steps in the first four measures below.

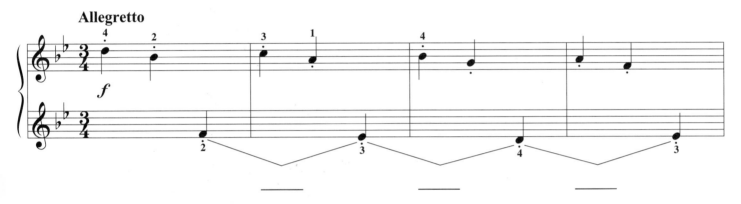

Name the circled triads in measures 9-14 below. Ex. C Major, c minor

1. _____

2. _____

3. _____

THE OLD GYPSY VIOLIN

Kevin Olson
(b. 1970)

Spotlight on Rests

rest — a sign of silence.

quarter rest
1 beat

half rest
2 beats

whole rest
rest for the entire measure
— the number of beats
depends on the
time signature.

Place a check next to the correct answers below.

In the last two measures of this composition there are a total of 8 rests.
Which of the following statements is true?

_____ 5 of the rests = 1 beat and
1 of the rests = 5 beats

_____ 5 of the rests = 1 beat and
2 of the rests = 4 beats

_____ 2 of the rests = 2 beats and
1 of the rests = 4 beats

The motive of this piece is circled in measure 1. Including the motive,
how many times does this motive repeat in the first two lines?

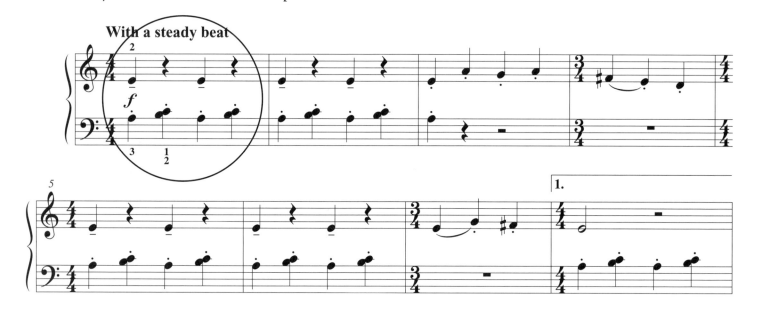

_____ 2 times

_____ 3 times

_____ 4 times

FJH2100

There are three types of articulations in measures 9 and 10 of this piece.
What are they? Check **three**.

_____ portato

_____ staccato

_____ legato

_____ tenuto

Is the pattern of whole and half steps in the R.H. in measures 10 and 14 the same or different?

_____ same

_____ different

Improvisation

1. Improvise in ⁵⁄₄ time, using the three hand positions suggested in line 1 below.
2. Start with the first two measures in line 2.
3. Keep going, and experiment with the given hand positions in different octaves.
4. Use your imagination!

Suggested hand positions

Start with these two measures

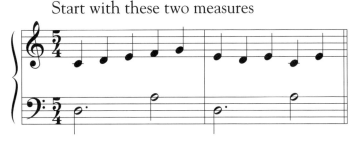

Keep going and have fun!

FJH2100

GLOSSARY OF MUSICAL TERMS

a tempo — return to the original tempo.

accent — emphasize the note. (See **signs**.)

accidental — a sharp, flat, or natural placed before a note.

Adagio — slow. (See **tempo**.)

Allegretto — a little fast. (See **tempo**.)

Allegro — fast and cheerful. (See **tempo**.)

Andante — walking speed. Moderately slow. (See **tempo**.)

articulation — the degree to which notes are separated or connected.

    legato — connected and smooth. Indicated by a slur:

    portato — halfway between *staccato* and *legato*. Indicated by this symbol:

    staccato — detached. Indicated by this symbol:

    tenuto — hold the notes for full value. Stress the note. Indicated by this symbol:

binary form — two-part form. (Found on page 28.)

clefs

    bass clef — play the notes on the lower half of the piano. Indicated by this symbol:

    treble clef — play the notes on the upper half of the piano. Indicated by this symbol:

common time = C — a symbol that stands for $\frac{4}{4}$ time. (See **time signature**.)

crescendo — gradually louder. (See **dynamics**.)

D.C. al Fine = *Da Capo al Fine* — Go back to the beginning and play to the *Fine* (end).

damper pedal — the pedal on the right that sustains the sound.

decrescendo — gradually softer. (See **dynamics**.)

diminuendo — gradually softer. (See **dynamics**.)

dolce — sweetly.

dominant — the 5th degree of a scale. (Found on pages 16 and 46.) (See **primary triads**.)

dotted half note — in $\frac{3}{4}$, $\frac{4}{4}$, and $\frac{5}{4}$ time, it receives 3 beats. (See **note and rest values**.)

dotted quarter note — in $\frac{2}{4}$, $\frac{3}{4}$, $\frac{4}{4}$, and $\frac{5}{4}$ time, it receives 1½ beats. (See **note and rest values**.)

dynamics — signs that indicate how loud or soft to play. (Found on pages 22 and 44.)

> *crescendo* — gradually louder (⟍).
>
> *decrescendo* and *diminuendo* — gradually softer (⟋).
>
> *forte* — loud (***f***).
>
> *fortissimo* — very loud (***ff***).
>
> *mezzo forte* — medium loud (***mf***).
>
> *mezzo piano* — medium soft (***mp***).
>
> *piano* — soft (***p***).
>
> *pianissimo* — very soft (***pp***).

eighth note — in $\frac{2}{4}$, $\frac{3}{4}$, $\frac{4}{4}$, and $\frac{5}{4}$ time, it receives ½ beat. (See **note and rest values**.)

eighth rest — in $\frac{2}{4}$, $\frac{3}{4}$, $\frac{4}{4}$, and $\frac{5}{4}$ time, it receives ½ beat of silence. (See **note and rest values**.)

-etto — little. (Found on page 34.)

fermata — a hold or pause. (See **signs**.)

Fine — the end.

first and second endings — (See **signs**.)

five-finger pattern — a certain pattern for the five fingers. (Found on pages 8, 36, and 58.)

flat — lower the note a ½ step. (See **accidental**.)

form

> binary form — two-part form. (Found on page 28.)
>
> ternary form — three-part form. (Found on page 52.)

forte — loud. (See **dynamics**.)

fortissimo — very loud. (See **dynamics**.)

half note — in $\frac{2}{4}$, $\frac{3}{4}$, $\frac{4}{4}$, and $\frac{5}{4}$ time, it receives 2 beats. (See **note and rest values**.)

half rest — in $\frac{2}{4}$, $\frac{3}{4}$, $\frac{4}{4}$, and $\frac{5}{4}$ time, it receives 2 beats of silence. (See **note and rest values**.)

half step — from one key to the closest key. (Found on page 4.)

harmony — chords: broken or blocked.

-ino — little. (Found on page 34.)

interval — the distance between two keys on the keyboard or two notes on the staff. (Found on pages 6, 38, and 64.)

key signature — the sharps or flats at the beginning of a composition that indicate the name of the scale that the composer used to write the music. (Found on pages 14, 31, and 48.)

Largo — very slow.

Larghetto — not quite as slow as *Largo*.

ledger lines — the lines above or below the staff. (See **staff notes**.)

legato — play connected and smooth. (See **articulation**.)

melody — an organized sequence of individual notes. (Found on pages 56 and 61.)

metronome marking — an indication of how fast to play the composition. (Found on page 62.)

mezzo forte — medium loud. (See **dynamics**.)

Moderato — medium or moderate tempo. (See **tempo**.)

molto — much.

motif — (See **motive**.)

motive — a small musical idea found at the beginning of a composition, which is found repeatedly throughout. (Found on pages 24, 42, and 54.)

natural — cancels a sharp or flat. (See **accidental**.)

non troppo — not too much.

notes — (See **note and rest values**.)

note and rest values

whole note	o	4 beats
whole rest	▬	rest the entire measure (2, 3, 4 or 5 beats)
half note	𝅗𝅥	2 beats
half rest	▬	2 beats
quarter note	𝅘𝅥	1 beat
quarter rest	𝄽	1 beat
eighth note	𝅘𝅥𝅮	½ beat

eighth rest	𝄾	½ beat
two eighth notes	♫	1 beat
dotted half note	𝅗𝅥.	3 beats
dotted quarter note	♩.	1½ beats

octave sign — play one octave higher or lower. (See **signs**.)

passing tone — a non-chord tone that passes between two chord tones.

ped. simile — continue to pedal in a similar manner.

pianissimo — very soft. (See **dynamics**.)

piano — soft. (See **dynamics**.)

più — more.

poco — little.

portato — halfway between *legato* and *staccato*. (See **articulation**.)

primary triads — triads built on the first (tonic), fourth (subdominant), and fifth (dominant) tones of a scale. They are the triads that are used most frequently in composition. (Found on pages 16 and 46.)

quarter note — in $\frac{2}{4}$, $\frac{3}{4}$, $\frac{4}{4}$, and $\frac{5}{4}$ time, it receives 1 beat. (See **note and rest values**.)

quarter rest — in $\frac{2}{4}$, $\frac{3}{4}$, $\frac{4}{4}$, and $\frac{5}{4}$ time, it receives 1 beat of silence. (See **note and rest values**.)

repeat sign — repeat. (See **signs**.)

rest — a sign of silence. (See **note and rest values**. Found on pages 29 and 66.)

retenu — a French musical term that means "retained" or "held back."

risoluto — resolved, determined, bold.

ritardando, rit. — gradually slower.

rhythm — a pattern of long and short note values in music. Everything pertaining to the length of a sound.

scale — a progression of notes in a certain order.

    Major scale — (Found on pages 18 and 30.)

sempre — always.

sharp — raise the note a ½ step higher. (See **accidental**.)

signs   accent — emphasize the note. 𝆖

        fermata — a hold or pause. 𝆒

first and second endings — play the first ending the first time, follow the repeat sign, then play the second ending the second time.

    | 1. | | 2. | |

octave sign — play one octave higher if the sign is placed above the notes.
Play one octave lower if the sign is placed below the notes.

slur — play connected and smooth. (See **articulation**.)

spiritoso — play in a spirited manner. (See **tempo**.)

staccato — detached. (See **articulation**.)

staff notes

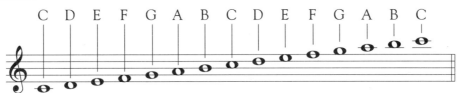

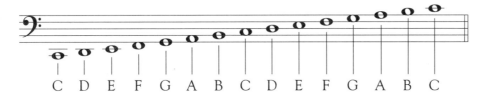

tempo — the speed at which a composition is played. (Found on pages 33 and 50.)

Adagio — slow.

Allegro — fast and cheerful.

Andante — walking speed.

Andantino — slightly faster than *Andante*.

Larghetto — not quite as slow as *Largo*.

Largo — very slow.

Moderato — moderate speed.

tenuto — hold the note for full value. Stress the note. (See **articulation**.)

ternary form — three-part form. (See **form**. Found on pages 52–53.)

tie — a curved line between notes of the same pitch that indicates to hold down both notes for their full value.

time signature — the upper number indicates the number of beats per measure. The lower number indicates what kind of note gets one beat. (Found on pages 10 and 60.)

$\frac{2}{4}$ $\frac{3}{4}$ $\frac{4}{4}$ $\frac{5}{4}$ — number of beats per measure
$\quad$ ♩ = one beat

tonic — the first degree of a scale. Also, a chord built on the first note of a scale. (Found on pages 16 and 46.) (See **primary triads**.)

triad — a chord with three tones. (Found on pages 20 and 40.)

whole note — in $\frac{4}{4}$ time, it receives 4 beats. (See **note and rest values**.)

whole rest — a rest that indicates silence for an entire measure. (See **note and rest values**.)

whole step — consists of two half steps. (Found on page 4.) (See **half and whole steps**.)